MENTORS: PRICELESS ADVISORS

(25 Examples)

By

Paul Rux, PH.D. (Wisconsin-Madison), M.A. (University of Toronto)
2018 Founding Mentor: ISEMP Mentorship Program -
University of Toronto / Ontario Institute for Studies in Education

Copyright 2018 by Paul Rux, Ph.D.

MENTORS: PRICELESS ADVISORS

"IN TRIBUTE TO AN ULTIMATE MENTOR"

ROBERT G. HEIDEMAN, Ph.D. (Wisconsin – Madison)

Founder and Director, Educational Placement & Career Services (Wisconsin-Madison)

"He saved lives."

Socrates taught out first step toward wisdom is to "know thyself, which means:

Know your gifts and talents. Respect and fully develop them.

Do not be the dancer who never danced, the writer who never wrote, or the teacher who never taught. Do not miss or dismiss yourself.

Socrates taught and applied this wisdom to help others. R.G. Heideman also applied it superbly.

R.G. Heideman dedicated his life to helping others to "know themselves" so they could "self-actualize" and have no regrets at the ends of their lives.

R.G. Heideman as a career and personal counselor – a mentor par excellence – helped others to "give themselves to themselves." There is no greater service to others. This writer knows. Heideman applied "know thyself" to me.

R.G. Heideman set the professional example that guides this writer's own work now as a mentor to help others to "know themselves" and "self-actualize" Heideman's Socratic "know thyself" examples is a "gift" that keeps on giving. It is also a par excellence example of mentoring. Thank you, Bob.

R.G. Heideman will be the first case study of mentoring in our book. He is a stellar mentoring example.

Paul Rux, Ph.D. (Wisconsin-Madison), Client of R.G. Heideman"

MENTORS VERSUS COACHES

In simplest terms, coaches command and mentors share. Think of coaching as formal, "vertical." The coach tells the player what to do and how to do it in the final analysis. In contrast, mentors advise others on how to improve. It is informal, "horizontal" sharing of insights between mentor and client. Mentoring does not involve commands. Rather it is reciprocal sharing of wisdom between friends.

FORMAL AND INFORMAL MENTORING

Mentoring can occur between persons as part of a formal program like the ISEMP Mentorship Program University of Toronto / Ontario Institute for Studies in Education, which I helped to launch in 2018 as one of its first Mentors. Its formality involves required monthly meetings between mentor and clients. The mentor and clients determine the subject matter for the meetings and share opinions about it. The mentor does not impose a right or wrong answer; in fact, the mentor encourages sharing of viewpoints among or between the mentor and the clients. It is fun, great, mutual learning through polite sharing.

MENTORS: PRICELESS ADVISORS

On the other hand, if the mentor seeks to impose an agenda on the client, we are now tutoring, not mentoring. Or call it coaching. Tutoring and coaching target grounding clients in specific skills and attitudes, not reciprocal crafting of information, skills, plans, attitudes or other negotiated needs. It is important to underscore the democratic nature of mentoring in comparison with coaching, tutoring.

PROOF OF THE POWER OF MENTORING

To show the reader the productive power of mentoring, I have selected sixteen examples of how mentoring has helped to shape my life path. As Aristotle observed, "our best lessons are caught from the examples of others, not from textbooks and lectures." Mentors provide such examples, and, in turn, we can provide them and others with priceless "life lessons" by examples and sharing "lessons learned." After reading each case study, reflect on how to apply its lessons to your own life and share them too.

CASE STUDY ONE: Robert Heideman, Ph.D. (Wisconsin - Madison)

In 1980, I was at summer school at Wisconsin – Madison, and on weekends I went home to Illinois, where my wife and I rented a house. One weekend, I got home and she announced our divorce and went right out of the door to her boyfriend's house.

When I got back to campus on Monday, I stumbled into the office of Robert Heideman, Director, Career Counseling, School of Education, Wisconsin – Madison. He told me to make no other decisions, go back to work for another school year, and then come to see him.

I did, and when we met a school year (9 months) later he had me talk for thirty minutes about my situation, feelings, and dreams, after which he said, "I see it now. You're going to get a Ph.D." "In what?" I asked. "Administration of Higher Education and Policy Analysis," he answered.

"Start with Prof. McCarty next month," he said. I listened and acted on his advice. In World War II, McCarty had been an army major on the staff of General Eisenhower. Heideman saw him as a role model for me, and I truly loved and learned from McCarty, as Heideman predicted.

Heideman next shared some of his own "lessons learned" to help me. He said his first wife blocked his dream to become a physician. The result was dropout from medical school, fivorceand the need to retool like me. He got his Ph.D. in Counseling, which enabled him to apply his heartfelt passion for helping others – like me. He also found a supportive wife. He knew exactly my needs from his own life.

It was stellar mentoring; the result is I have been a professor in higher education since 1994 and have won awards from doctoral students for being "best professor." Heideman has died, but I stay in touch with his widow so we can get together to celebrate his memory – his loving, timely, mentoring of others.

PERSONAL APPLICATION: How does this case study remind you of mentoring events in your life? Please briefly cite five examples for possible discussion.

1.

2.

MENTORS: PRICELESS ADVISORS

3.

4.

5.

CASE STUDY TWO: Jim Leonhardt, AT&T Lobbyist for the State of Wisconsin

This example of mentoring occurred within the past year of writing this book. It happened at a local hospital where I had gone for testing. To my surprise, my old friend Jim Leonhardt, retired state lobbyist for AT&T, was there for testing also. The testing was thorough and lasted for two weeks. Both of us lived in a special ward for clients who required extensive testing, which gave us a chance to renew our friendship, which had started when we collaborated to bring the Internet to rural Wisconsin.

I worked for the Southwest Wisconsin Library System, SWLS, which had its base in Fennimore, Wisconsin, 1992-1998, to design and deploy a $1-million Internet project to connect twenty –eight public libraries across five rural counties in Southwest Wisconsin to Internet services. For my work, I won awards from the Wisconsin State Telecommunications Association, Governor, and Legislature.

The project centered on telecommunications, and this is how I met Jim Leonhardt. AT&T provides the backbone of long distance connectivity for telecommunications across Wisconsin, and Internet cannot occur without such a backbone. It was a delight to team with him to move Wisconsin into the future.

Given the size and complexity of the project, we were not always able to maintain a strict timeline. One of the library directors used this to blackmail my boss to give his library free access or he would report our timetable delay to a major project donor, Lands' End, Dodgeville, Wisconsin. It had donated $75,000 to us, since it wanted it workforce to be able to practice computing skills during leisure time in local libraries, for these skills had direct value to the company's workplace. Now it faced blackmail.

My boss told me of this threat, and I called Jim Leonhardt immediately. Jim, of course, knew the reasons for timeline delays as one of the backbone service providers, and he called the VP of operations at Lands' End, a client and friend of his too. Jim explained the delay and defused the blackmail threat.

Later, I confronted the blackmailer at the monthly meeting of System members. That ended the blackmail and the blackmailer's job. It also created a special friendship between Jim and me, and we were glad to be able to visit again, even if it happened in a hospital ward. We both loved the chance.

During one of our visits in his room, Jim mentored me – by surprise! He said, "Paul, at this point in our lives we must, first, "face facts" and, second, we must define our "legacy." Thank you, Jim Leonhardt, for your surprise, timely, targeted mentoring of me. Yes, we "seniors" need to face new facts about about our health, finances, and need for friendship and family, and rethink how to meet them. I never, ever expected this kind of profound mentoring in a hospital; I thank Jim Leonhardt for it. In time, we have agreed to collaborate on a book about lobbying, during which we can mentor each other more.

MENTORS: PRICELESS ADVISORS

PERSONAL APPLICATION: How does this case study remind you of mentoring events in your life? Please briefly cite five examples for possible discussion.

1.

2.

3.

4.

5.

CASE STUDY THREE: Prof. David Andrew Thornley, Ph.D., University of Dublin, Ireland

As Aristotle observed, "the best lessons are caught from the examples of others, not through lectures and reading books." This applies to the example of Prof. David Andrew Thornley, Ph.D., University of Dublin, Ireland, for the need to have courage to support what is right, not what is career expedient.

I was a student of Thornley in his one-year course on the history of political science at the University as a special one-year student in the Honours School of History and Political Science at the University of Dublin, 1964-1965. Our course met one weekly for two hours for the academic year. Thornley caught our interest with creative insights into the historical roots of political science and how we could apply them now. He "walked his talk" as he planned to run for the Irish Parliament for the Labour Party.

Thornley was an impressive blend of theory and practice; he won and held our respect because of his scholarly wisdom, insights into how to apply it, and his being faculty advisor to the University's student boxing club, of which he was an award-winning member when he was a student at the University. In fact, his "flattened nose" from his days in the ring was a badge of honor that further enhanced his respect with us students. Yet, he insisted we wear our black academic robes, Oxford style, to class, and expected courtly behavior in class. He knew how to blend values, social, academic, and political.

I had a stunning example of his ability to blend values as I watched the Irish TV network program "Meet the Professor," which aired once weekly, in the spring of 1965. Winston Churchill had died; the U.K. went into mourning and raised its flags in tribute to him. Churchill after World War I was Home Secretary and negotiated the treaty that separated Ulster from the Republic of Ireland. For this many Irish never forgave him. The proof of this hatred of him exploded in Ireland with his death. As the British raised their flags to honor Churchill, the Irish raised their flags to protest hisnegotiating the treaty that split six counties from the Republic of Ireland to form the Province of Ulster in the United Kingdom.

At the time, one third of our enrollment at the University was from the U.K. During the night, to protest the Irish protest, these British students took down the Irish flags at the University and replaced them with British flags! Of course, this caused an explosion of anger across Ireland which found its way onto Irish national TV. In short, Thornley's "Meet the Professor" interview happened in the middle of this

MENTORS: PRICELESS ADVISORS

burst of anger on TV over Churchill and the flags at the University. Naturally, the host of the show asked Thornely about it. Here was a man who wanted to be a member of the Irish Parliament and needed Irish votes; therefore, his answer completely surprised and awed me – to this day. It went like this:

"When I was age 11, I was in Manchester England with my parents at the start of World War II. My father held a factory war job. I recall going into the air raid shelters at night when the bombing attacks came, the lights went out, the ground shook, and Churchill came on the radio to give us hope.

We Irish must always remember we are part of Western Civilization, and when it faced its darkest moments because of Hitler, Churchill stood between us and Histler's total evil. Despite our differences with Churchill, we must consider the 'big picture' and move ahead."

Wow, Thornley had courage, despite his own ambitions, to stand firmly for the right. He has remained an example for how I want to be in such situations. He really mentored me, and he did not know it! Thank you, Dr. Thornley, who did get elected to the Irish Parliament and sadly died at age forty-two.

Yes, this example of Dr. Thornley, Churchill, and I shows how mentoring can be "caught, not taught."

PERSONAL APPLICATION: How does this case study remind you of mentoring events in your life? Please briefly cite five examples for possible discussion.

1.

2.

3.

4.

5.

CASE STUDY FOUR: Dalton Camp, PR Director, Conservative Party of Canada

In 1975-76, I was a history, political science, and world religions teacher at Loyalist Collegiate and Vocational Institute, LCVI, at Kingston, Ontario, Canada. Before Loyalist, I had taught such subjects at the District High School, Wiarton, Ontario, Canada, 1971-1975. Before Wiarton, I had taught them at Saint Andrew's College, Aurora, Ontario, 1970-1971, as a replacement teacher for a House Master on leave. Thus, it is fair to say I arrived at Loyalist as an experienced, dedicated classroom teacher

At LCVI, I received a surprise mentoring lesson which has guided me to this day. Here is how it happened. In the fall, the social studies teachers in the region held their annual professional development conference in Kingston. The guest speaker was Dalton Camp, PR Director for the Conservative Party of Canada. For some reason, I received the honor to have lunch with Camp, his wife, and another teacher after Camp's keynote presentation. I had no idea Camp would mentor us at lunch about the future of politics, government in North America which still applies today, sadly.

MENTORS: PRICELESS ADVISORS

First, the other teacher at our table asked Camp how a boy from New Brunswick ends up being PR Director for the Conservative Party of Canada. Camp (Canadian World War II veteran) answered, "Well, I was in Europe and people were shooting at me" (World War II). I wondered why, and I figured out the shooters had experienced institutional failure. I resolved that if I survived the war, I would come home to Canada to make sure that our people never lost faith in our institutions."

As I write this in 2018, I am keenly aware of the increasing risks for institutional failure for American government today. Camp alerted me to such a danger, whether German, Canadian, or American. Hopefully, we avoid it, I pray.

Second, in fairness to the second teacher at our table, Camp asked me what was on my mind. I answered, "What is the future of politics in North America." I had just joined the World Future Society, WFS, to which I still belong, and my question reflected my new WFS interest. Camp replied, "We foresee the death of the middle class in North America. What this means yet for politics we do not yet know; it is not likely good."

Wow, Camp described in 1975 what is happening exactly in 2018 as I type this. Camp shared his wisdom with me informally, without testing, preparatory reading, or lecturing. It was ideal mentoring format. Above all, it contained "lessons learned" from a frontline expert. Camp died in 2002; his mentoring insights to me in 1975 apply yet today. Thank you, Dalton, for the mentoring.

PERSONAL APPLICATION: How does this case study remind you of mentoring events in your life? Please briefly cite five examples for possible discussion.

1.

2.

3.

4.

5.

CASE STUDY FIVE: Ted Mayer, Teacher, Loyalist Collegiate and Vocational Institute, Kingston, Ontario

One of the surprises and blessings at Loyalist when I arrived as a new teacher there in 1975 was Ted Mayer. Ted was a vocational ("shop") teacher. He and his wife lived on the road to our rental house just outside Kingston, and Ted became a surprise mentor for me at a crucial moment in my career.

First, Ted was a German immigrant. He had fought in World War II in the German Army on the Eastern Front against the Russians and was wounded three times. He paid a price for this with our students who constantly greeted him with insults like "Heil Hitler, Sieg Heil, and Achtung." I never saw him respond to such insults; sadly, the school administrators did nothing to stop the abuse.

MENTORS: PRICELESS ADVISORS

My ancestors were Prussian, my parents both spoke German at home, as did my other family members. I could relate to his immigrant status, for our family had similar abuses during World War I. As a result, I ate lunch with him at school and we became friends, which was a wise move on my part because of how the school year would unfold. It also gave me insight into Germany history under Hitler.

One key mentoring insight, as Ted shared, 25% of German men were unemployed and lived on the streets as a result of the Great Depression. They were desperate; Hitler appealed to their desperation.

For example, the Nazi Storm Troopers recruited members by providing men living on the streets with beds, clean clothes, food and a form of respect. It was about basic survival, not politics, for most of them. Of course, this is not what war propaganda portrays.

Second, Ted lived in constant fear of another Great Depression, and he constantly wrote letters to newspapers about the dangers of deficit spending and inflation. He had experienced the brutal results such financial trickery can explode. Our lunches included mentoring which still has, sadly, validity today.

Third, Ted's mentoring became crucial when the head of the history department began to fear my successes as steps toward overthrowing him. For instance, I fielded a student delegation of six to the national conference of the Conservative Party of Canada in nearby Ottawa for a weekend. The field study became local newspaper news and caused my boss to panic about his job security.

My goal was to win tenure so I could study part-time on a Ph.D. at Queen's University in Kingston, the second top university in Ontario, after Toronto. My boss perceived it otherwise.

As a result, tension grew between us; I told Ted about it. Ted advised me to get out of Loyalist and return to America. He said, "You're too big for Loyalist or even Canada. Go back." I had been in Canada for eight years; it was a surprise to get this advice. However, I did return in 1976, and as I type this, I thank Ted Mayer for his support, advice, and mentoring. It came at a "tipping point."

I had come to Canada to resist the Vietnam War. I had not been home in eight years. Now, with the war over and amnesty in place for my case (I am a conscientious objector) I could go home. I figured, if Ted Mayer could immigrate to Canada as a former German soldier after World War II, I could return to America from exile after the Vietnam War. Ted mentored and gave me courage to act. Thank you, Ted.

PERSONAL APPLICATION: How does this case study remind you of mentoring events in your life? Please briefly cite five examples for possible discussion.

1.

2.

3.

4.

5.

MENTORS: PRICELESS ADVISORS

CASE STUDY SIX: Neil Giffey, My Dodgeville, Wisconsin, Mentor

I lived in Dodgeville, Wisconsin, 1992-1998, while I was a technology planner for the Southwest Wisconsin Library System, which encompassed the five counties between Madison, Wisconsin and Dubuque, Iowa. During my stay in Dodgeville, I met Neil Giffey, who recruited me to the local Kiwanis as a way to overcome my isolation as a newcomer, make friends, and provide services to the locals.

He and I also became personal friends, for we shared a passion for history; the letter below describes his fabulous award-winning skills as a writer of history and champion of history resources like museums.

Neil mentored me about how to "fit in" to Dodgeville, write for publication and fun, and serve others. None of this was formal learning. Rather, it was informal sharing, mentoring. Below is a letter to Neil Giffey's widow from me. It captures my love for him and his mentoring me. Thank you, Neil.

"April 26, 2018

Dear Jan and Family:

I often think of Neil and how he has set an example for me to be of help to others. Thank you, Neil!

I also believe Neil's memory deserves honor. I am thinking of how the Dodge County Historical Society could create an annual Neil Giffey Day on which it would present Neil Giffey awards to its outstanding members and others in the area who have advanced the cause of local history as Neil did so splendidly.

It could involve certificates, trophies, newspaper stories, radio interviews with prize winners, and many other forms of recognition. I am sure you and your family can craft ones of special meaning to you.

I recall how I got Governor Martin Schreiber to present Neil with an award in the state capitol for Neil's outstanding local history work with special recognition for his Henry Dodge historical research, writing.

The Kiwanis may also want to support a Neil Giffey Day, since he was also an outstanding Kiwanian. I really want to preserve his memory as an example of how others can build on his strong foundations.

I hope this does not surprise you too much. I, too, am now writing, and Neil is my model for how to do it. For instance, I also listen to the Wisconsin Public Radio classical radio station. Thank you, Neil!

Please let me know if I can be of help with this in some way. However, I am sure you know persons who worked closely with Neil with local history who can add lots of ideas and support for this.

Again, God blessed me when He crossed Neil's life path with mine. I love, honor, and miss him. I want to live up to his standards as best I can. I hope, pray you will act on this proposal. Neil deserves it.

God bless you and yours,

Paul Rux, Ph.D."

MENTORS: PRICELESS ADVISORS

(At this time of writing for this book, I have not received a reply to this letter. However, I am hoping.)

PERSONAL APPLICATION: How does this case study remind you of mentoring events in your life? Please briefly cite five examples for possible discussion.

1.

2.

3.

4.

5.

CASE STUDY SEVEN: John Johnson, Wiarton, Ontario, Surprise Mentor in a "Snow Bank"

John Johnson was the guidance counselor at the District High School in Wiarton, Ontario, where I worked as a history and English teacher 1971-1975. Wiarton, population 1,600, sits on the shores of the Bruce Peninsula, which juts from Southern Ontario seventy miles into Georgian Bay, an inlet of Lake Huron. Wiarton averaged 184 inches of snow yearly; which reduced travel to and from Wiarton during the winter months. As a result, Wiartonians turned to each other for social life, fun, and friendships.

This isolation benefited me because it gave me a chance to become friends with John Johnson, one of the top mentors in my lifetime to date. He was lonesome for intellectual friendship; I was too.

We were a perfect match, and on Friday nights after supper I would walk three blocks over to his house, where we would sit in the living room, often with cans of beer, to discuss the issues of the day.

John read journals like *The Atlantic* and was always eager to get my opinion of his "take" on articles in such intellectual publications. We always had two hours of Friday night fun, during which he often mentored me with his own "rich" life experiences.

For instance, John grew up in Sudbury, Ontario, a major mining center. He started life in the mines until World War II made him a door gunner on a Canadian bomber flying out of England to bomb Germany. After the war, he got a veteran's benefit to earn his degrees at the University of British Columbia in Vancouver; John remained a rural Ontarian at heart and returned to become high school counselor in Wiarton, Ontario, which is how I met him.

I had just come from the campus of the University of Toronto and welcomed an intellectual "friend" like John. In fact, on my first day on the job, the staff hooted and laughed at my "nicey-nicey" British-style campus clothing; I never wore it again in Wiarton, ever. The sons and daughters of miners had no time for fake social class; I thank them for the reality check. I still know how to "fake" clothing but don't. I thank the men and women of Wiarton District High School for this precious, loving, reality check.

MENTORS: PRICELESS ADVISORS

John, because of his mining background, had a strong, personal interest in working-class politics, the New Democrats party in Canada, a spin-off of the British Labor Party. I saluted them for making it possible for Canada to have "socialized" medicine for all Canadians, and Canadian immigrants like me.

Graduated income taxes paid for the comprehensive system of medical treatment for all Canadians; the waiter and cook at MacDonald's had access to the same care as did the richest stock broker on Bay Street, Toronto (the second largest stock exchange after New York in North America). It was because of men like John that Canadians have medical justice. It is painful to observe the cancerous greed running and ruining equitable medical care in the U.S.A. in comparison.

John also had a delightful fun side. When school ended, he and his wife launched their sailboat and disappeared on the Great Lakes for three months. They returned just in time for the start of school.

John loved to tell stories about how they would tie up in fancy yacht clubs in places like Chicago. As the sailboat owners and their passengers would socialize, sooner or later it would "slip out" that he was a Socialist from Canada. He laughed about the disbelief this caused in the Americans around him. How could a working man have a sail boat, be a Socialist, and have money left over for a middle class life?

Yes, John, you gave me priceless lessons about social justice through your examples and insights. For instance, your stories about the mining strikes in which you took part as a young man have been a great form of mentoring about priorities in life for me. I know you have passed physically, but I believe you still find ways to sail the Great Lakes to tease and taunt capitalist "bloodsuckers." Keep sailing!

PERSONAL APPLICATION: How does this case study remind you of mentoring events in your life? Please briefly cite five examples for possible discussion.

1.

2.

3.

4.

5.

CASE STUDY EIGHT: Pastor Bruno Ederma, Wiarton, Ontario, Canada, Surprise Estonian Mentor

One of my surprises, and blessing, during my four years in Wiarton, Ontario, Canada, 1971-1975, where I taught high school, was being able to belong to St. Peter's Lutheran Church there, which is how I met Pastor Bruno Ederma. a wise, tested mentor, who knew how to share his wisdom with others. For the record, I was also the church organist during my time at St. Peter's, which gave me a chance to interact with Pastor Ederma on a regular basis as we planner for different services, e.g. a service in the Estonian language. Yes, Pastor Ederma was a refugee from Estonia, who, like me, "landed" in Canada.

MENTORS: PRICELESS ADVISORS

It was time for the sermon in the worship service format. Pastor Ederma picked up the Bible from the altar, and turned around to face the congregation with it. "This is a Bible. It is important for many have given their lives for believing its teachings. For example, the bishop who ordained me was shot to death because he believed in this book. My name was on the same list. This is why we hold its teachings sacred. Amen." I shall never forget this sermon and its message about what counts and can happen.

Pastor's example, of course, was a by-product of the Russian Communist conquest of Estonia at the start of World War II. Pastor fled to Germany as a refugee; after the war ended he ended up in a refugee camp in Denmark. From there, he found his way to America, and from there he came to Canada.

It is hard to "fool" somebody like him with idealistic, dumb talk, which sadly permeates much of higher education and the mass media today, at least in the USA. As an example of such fantasy propaganda, Pastor mentioned how his generation embraced the League of Nations of President Woodrow Wilson as the end to war among countries. "We were better off under the rule of the Czar" he told me. He knew.

Our small parish, had sixty-six members. This made it easy for us to socialize. For example, we could have picnics. Or we could have a Christmas party in our church basement.

At one of the Christmas party, Pastor Ederma stood up with an organge help up in one hand. Everybody stopped talking and turned to listen to him. This is what he said:

"When we arrived in New York City from our refugee camp in Denmark after World War II, it was Christmas Eve. The only gift we had was an orange, which I peeled and shared with my family members. As I shared the organge with them, I said, 'Merry Christmas, we are still alive. Thank you Jesus.'"

Privately, Pastor Ederma urged me to continue my studies for the ministry, which I had started in America at McCormcik Theological Seminary in Chicago, IL, before my draft board violated my First Amendment rights to draft me for Vietnam in violation of "Separation of Church and State." It was a hard choice; I made it. Pastor knew it, and he was no friend of Communism. He honored my choice. His last words to me as I got ready to move to Kingston, Ontario were "Always obey your conscience."

Two years after leaving Wiarton, word came to us of his death. God blessed me in Wiarton with him. I Thank you, Pastor Ederma, for sharing your "lessons learned" about reality. I shall never forget you.

PERSONAL APPLICATION: How does this case study remind you of mentoring events in your life? Please briefly cite five examples for possible discussion.

1.

2.

3.

4.

5.

MENTORS: PRICELESS ADVISORS

CASE STUDY NINE: Hal Moore, Tarrytown, New York, Surprise Mentor in a Wheelchair

After returning to America from Canada, I became a librarian. I earned my M.A.L.S. (Master's in Library Science) at the University of Wisconsin – Madison.

I worked as a K-12 school librarian for twelve years. Two of them were at the Masters School, Dobbs Ferry, New York, which hired me to help it keep its state certification. I had helped to certify five school libraries in Illinois during the eight years before the offer from Masters came, and my own K-12 library system won the annual award for most improved school library system in the State of Illinois.

It was through Masters School that I met my next mentor, Hal Moore, a victim of polio who lived in a wheelchair on welfare in nearby Tarrytown, New York on the Hudson River, upstream from Dobbs Ferry.

Over the years, I had learned to make friends with janitors, who serve as an intelligence system for they hear a lot and read a lot on desks as they quietly go about their jobs. One of my janitor friends said I ought to meet Hal Moore, too, for he could teach me a lot about New York City area because of his career before polio retired him to a wheelchair. I agreed, and I got a fabulous new mentor, Hal Moore.

I told Hal that I was tiring of K-12 teaching and school librarianship and wanted some other options. Hal had been a marketing guru in Manhattan with a specialization in political campaigns. Therefore, he suggested my exploring job options in politics. Hal had the connections; he shared them with me.

First, Hal introduced me to Andrew J. Spano, Register of Deeds for Westchester County, New York, the "Golden Apple" that has corporate money like IBM's international headquarters in it. I told Spano I wanted to work with colleges and universities to have them create and sponsor business incubators. We shopped the idea around Westchester; campus pensioners only had interest in teaching, not jobs.

Second, Hal arranged for me to attend a private meeting with Bob Kerry, Governor of Nebraska, who was running for President. The meeting was held on the west side of Central Park in the Dakota Department House where John Lennon and Yoko Ono had lived! In fact, Lennon was "gunned down" at the gate as he returned to his apartment there. Bill Clinton was also in town fundraising the same night; Clinton of course got the nomination; Kerry did not. Therefore, Hal further use of his network for me.

Third, the next "job interview" for me was to attend a private "deep pocket" fundraiser for Michael Dukakis who also was running for President. Hal had connections to get me invited to such events although I had no money to donate. It was a chance to network with campaign managers to explore chances for campaign and staff jobs. Again, Clinton bumped aside candidates like Dukakis. The result was a growing decision on my part to return to Wisconsin, my home state, to resume Ph.D. studies.

Hal Moore impressed on me the importance of connections. "Who sent you?" In this case, Hal Moore sent me; he opened doors to powerful networks of opportunities. In exchange for Hal's mentoring, I took him to football games at West Point Military Academy which was just twenty-five miles up the Hudson River from Tarrytown and Dobbs Ferry. Because of his wheelchair, we even got to sit on the playing field beyond the goal posts. Yet, Hal advised me to go back to the Midwest. I was not getting career traction in New York. I listened, and I thank him for his loving lesson: Yes, "Who sent you?"

MENTORS: PRICELESS ADVISORS

I cannot leave Hal Moore without sharing his last phone call to me. As he advised, I was back in the Midwest, working as an IT planner, and living in Dodgeville, Wisconsin, the home of Lands' End, a huge clothing company. Lands' End at the time leveraged its beautiful rural Wisconsin scenery setting in its advertising, print and electronic. Hal saw one of the ads on TV, and he called and in an excited voice said, "If that is where you live, don't you ever leave there." Amen, Hal. I agree with you.

I took my wife Jane to visit Hal, and we found him in bed in Tarrytown. His wheelchair days were over; his life was also coming to an end. It was hard, but I was thankful to be able to thank him again.

PERSONAL APPLICATION: How does this case study remind you of mentoring events in your life? Please briefly cite five examples for possible discussion.

1.

2.

3.

4.

5.

CASE STUDY TEN: Prof. John Sargent Moir, University of Toronto

One of the great experiences of my life has been being the student of John Moir at the University of Toronto, 1970-1971. Moir was Canada's great Church historian, and he offered a one-year course on the history of Canadian religious traditions. Having been in a seminary in Chicago before moving to Canada, it was an obvious choice for me as part of my Toronto M.A. program.

To my surprise, only two students were in the course, myself and a woman from Montreal. She and I met with Prof. Moir once weekly for two hours. It was pure "Oxford style." Prof. Moir gave us a topic, asked us to research it in the library, and create a two-page report on our findings for our next class.

In effect, Moir was being the classic Oxford "reader," who read research reports but did not "dump" information on students as his primary function. Wow, I have never had a better approach to learning!

Moreover, Moir took a personal interest in us. For instance, I had the flu during the winter. I had to stay home. He called to ask how I was doing! I cannot recall this happening with any other teacher.

Or, my weight dropped to 145 pounds (it is now 210), and Moir called my wife to express his concerns about my health. The weight loss was due to stress from moving to Canada due to the Vietnam War.

Furthermore, Moir considered his grad students to be part of his family. As a result, my wife and I received an invitation to join his wife and him at their home for a Christmas party with one other student and another professor and his wife. No professor ever has done this except for J.F.C. Harrison, my British history professor at Wisconsin – Madison, who, in fact, was from the U.K., a Cambridge alum.

MENTORS: PRICELESS ADVISORS

My research paper for Moir won accolades. I focused on the early history of the English-speaking Catholic Church in Ontario, called Canada West at the time. The Canadian Church Historical Society asked for its presentation at its annual conference at Quebec that year. This is truly a student honor!

Because of my work with him for 1970-71, Prof. Moir asked me to get my Ph.D. with him to continue to build on my course paper for him. He and his wife invited me and my wife to their home and he asked my wife, "If I get Paul a fellowship and a teaching assistantship, will you support his being my Ph.D. student?" My wife said, "No." She wanted a house, and this tension eventually destroyed our marriage.

Although I ended up getting my Ph.D. from Wisconsin – Madison, after divorcing my first wife, I always kept in touch with Prof. Moir. I would visit when we were in his area. I would give him updates on my studies, and he would update me on his situation. During our last visit, Prof. Moir took me aside into his private library in his home and said, "Paul, please do this for me. Do a study on the future of religion in Canada. Immigration is going to change this country forever; with it, religious traditions will change too." I promised, and it is a promise that I plan to keep. Call it my substitute Ph.D. dissertation for him.

My new wife reminds me of his final message to us as we got into our car to leave, "Paul, listen to what Jane says. You have no common sense." Again, Prof. Moir "hit the nail on the head" good and hard.

Prof. Moir subsequently died of kidney failure; his example and love for me continues. Thank you. I intend to complete the study of the future of religion in his honor and memory. It's a work of love.

PERSONAL APPLICATION: How does this case study remind you of mentoring events in your life? Please briefly cite five examples for possible discussion.

1.

2.

3.

4.

5.

CASE STUDY ELEVEN: Victor C. Last, Geography Teacher and Entrepreneur, Wiarton, Ontario, Canada

I had the good fortune to meet, know, and work with Victor Last while I was a teacher at the District High School in Wiarton, Ontario, Canada. It had 300 students on average, and this helped to stifle the need and funds for stifling bureaucracies that sadly hamstring progress, innovation, and esprit de corps among teachers and staff. One result was the school's capacity to attract and keep Victor C. Last as its geography teacher, one of the most creative persons and teachers to ever cross my path to date.

Victor told me he started teaching in Ottawa, Ontario, Canada's capital city and his hometown. However, his creativity posed a threat to the bureaucrats in charge of operations, and he had to go. Fortunately, he found Wiarton, a small town of 1,600 on the shore of Georgian Bay of Lake Huron.

MENTORS: PRICELESS ADVISORS

Doug Nickel, principal of the high school there, valued artisan teachers, and he hired Victor. It is also one of the reasons why he hired me, for he gave me scope to create and teach new first-ever courses like World Religions and Native American studies in addition to update my Canadian history and grade 9 English course, which included basic literature and the fundamentals of writing. For teacher creativity, the high school in Wiarton was the place to be. It treated us as artisans, not assembly line machines. Nickel and Wiarton spoiled me, for they gave proof that teaching can and should be artistic, creative.

Here is an example of Victor Last's creativity. He had students draw maps of the Wiarton area. Then, he took them out to the local airport, where they boarded a plane, with their maps in hand. The plane took off and Victor asked the students once they were in the air to compare how their maps with what they saw below them from the airplane. I have never seen, or heard of a better teaching method than this!

Every summer Victor would travel literally to a different part of the world, where he would take photos to create slides for a special set of drawers in his classroom. This is how it worked. For example, he would tell students to go to drawer C, which had Cuban slides that he had arranged by various topics. Then he would ask the students to view the slides, for instance, on transportation and craft a report on transportation in Cuba for their deductive analysis of information. It was pure scientific method; he used it over and over to instill scientific method in his students. It does not get better than this. Believe me.

Victor also applied his creativity to the Wiarton community. When he arrived, it had no postcards. Victor fixed this, and Wiarton now has color and historical postcards because of him. He even turned parts of the old mansion of a lumber baron that Victor had purchased into a small video theater, since downtown Wiarton had lost its commercial movie theater due to ugly alcoholic misbehavior in it.

Yes, Ottawa's loss was Wiarton's gain. Victor's lesson to me in a nutshell has been: innovation occurs on the flexible edges, not at the ossified centers. (We call this the "Theory of Complex Numbers," or the "Butterfly Effect," first presented in 1963 by Edward Lorenz.) We have kept in touch over the years; I am still always amazed with his ongoing creativity. For instance, during our last visit to his mansion, he showed us his new museum, which houses artifacts he found in his mansion, in and on its grounds.

Over the years, Victor has mentored me with lessons about creativity and how it is likely to occur. Yes, if you want to hatch the next new product or service, consider small, not large, settings to launch it.

PERSONAL APPLICATION: How does this case study remind you of mentoring events in your life? Please briefly cite five examples for possible discussion.

1.

2.

3.

4.

5.

MENTORS: PRICELESS ADVISORS

CASE STUDY TWELVE: Rev. C. August Hardt, D.D., Concordia College, Milwaukee, Wisconsin

In 1958, I started grade nine at boarding high school at Concordia College in Milwaukee, Wisconsin. The boarding school has closed, but my memories of its values continue to mentor my choices. An example of one of these memory values is my Old Testament Professor C. August Hardt, D.D. He was our grade nine Old Testament teacher, and the course ran for the entire academic year. In grade 10, we studied the New Testament with another professor, and in grade 11 we studied the Catechism of Martin Luther with another professor for another academic year. Concordia made sure we got our foundations.

At the end of my grade nine year, Prof. Hardt retired from teaching to be a chaplain in a Lutheran home for the aged in Milwaukee. I never saw him again. This is why a surprise letter from him to me twelve years later when I was living in Canada has made such a huge impression on me. His letter is a stellar example of student-teacher loyalty in the best tradition of great teachers like Confucius and Lao-Tzu.

I was teaching in Wiarton, Ontario, Canada, starting in 1972. I had left America for Canada in 1968 to protest the draft for the Vietnam War as a conscientious objector. I offered medical service, but my draft board refused it. Moreover, I was enrolled in a seminary, McCormick Theological Seminary, in Chicago to study for the ministry – on scholarship; thus, drafting me violated my separation-of-church-and-state First Amendment rights in the U.S. Constitution. However, my draft board had political grudges against my mother; we could not afford the court costs. Canada emerged as the right option.

Picture this. I have not seen or heard from Prof. Hardt since 1959. It is now 1972, and a letter to me from him finds me in Canada. I opened it, and it read, "If you are Paul Rux, my student, then I know you are doing the right thing. God bless you, Dr. Hardt." I could not believe what I was reading. First, he had to find out my legal situation. Second, he had to find out my Canadian mailing address. Third, he took special effort to reaffirm the classic, forever loyal bond between us as teacher and student. Dr. Hardt taught me, mentored me, how teacher-student relationships are more than subject matter and grading. It involves personal caring for each other, which ought to be lifetime. He really mentored me.

PERSONAL APPLICATION: How does this case study remind you of mentoring events in your life? Please briefly cite five examples for possible discussion.

1.

2.

3.

4.

5.

CASE STUDY THIRTEEN: Zona Gale (1874-1938), Portage, Wisconsin

I never met Zona Gale personally. I, however, experienced her legacy, which helped to mentor me to become the person I am. Zona Gale and I share the same hometown, Portage, Wisconsin. She was born

MENTORS: PRICELESS ADVISORS

there, and I grew up there. My parents moved to Portage in 1945 from Montello, Wisconsin to open a beauty shop in the downtown hotel in Portage. The shop still runs under a different name and family.

Growing up in Portage without learning about Zona Gale is almost impossible. The public library when I was a boy there was her gift of her own home to Portage for such use. I spent summers, weekends, and many days after school in her gift public library. It even had saved her office; when we were old enough we were allowed to go inside to look at it for a few minutes.

Because of Zona's gift, I developed a love of libraries, which, in turn, led to my earning a M.A.L.S. (Master's in Library Science) from the University of Wisconsin – Madison, which was Zona's alma mater too. I then pursued a career in librarianship for twenty years before switching to university work. In fact, for my M.A.L.S. thesis, I researched and wrote a paper on "Zona Gale and Public Libraries."

The Governor Wisconsin in the 1920's, the great Progressive Robert M. La Follette appointed Zona to be chair of the state's Public Library Commission's board out of respect for her advocacy of public libraries. My research found Zona backed public libraries because they provided meeting spaces and places for all social classes in a community to come together to meet each other as they used library services.

When I read this, my admiration for Zona skyrocketed even higher! Although she was part of the upper class of Portage, through marriage to the richest man in town, and her own professional achievements, she cared about preventing toxic class divisions as the Industrial Revolution hit Portage hard after World War I. In effected, Zona mentored me about a core value of public libraries and librarianship through her legacy to my hometown. My respect for her went to greater heights than her 1920 Pulitzer Prize.

My mother, an "immigrant" to Portage, was able to join the Women's Civic League, which met in the home of Zona Gale's parents on the banks of the Wisconsin River. Zona had built the small, white mansion for her parents, and after they died, she donated it to the Women's Civic League for the same reason she donated her own home for a library. She wanted ample social space for members of all social classes in Portage to meet each other to overcome class divisions and to create caring community.

My mother's membership is a perfect example of Gale's vision for the clubhouse. Mother in effect was an "immigrant" to Portage, but the Women's Civic League helped to integrate her into the community. After she died, the League invited me to give a memorial address for my mother to them. The core of it centered on Zona's famous best-seller *Friendship Village,* which celebrates community, not class war.

Again, the clubhouse for the Women's Civic League and the mansion for the public library from Zona Gale as resources to Portage to avoid class divisions and loss of community unity indirectly mentored me, my values, which I hold dear to this day. It is amazing how such legacies can mentor us, shape our values, and nurture our moral health as an individual, community, and society. God bless Zona Gale.

PERSONAL APPLICATION: How does this case study remind you of mentoring events in your life? Please briefly cite five examples for possible discussion.

1.

MENTORS: PRICELESS ADVISORS

2.

3.

4.

5.

CASE STUDY FOURTEEN: Emil Rux, Portage, Wisconsin

As Aristotle observed, our best "lessons" are "caught" from the examples of others, not taught through lectures and textbooks. This logic applies perfectly to my father, who has mentored me in many ways through his actions which still guide my life. Research today tells us too many children are started for this kind of mentoring. One third of American children live in single parent homes. Another third of them have parents who both work. Thus, only one third of children today in America receive the kind of parental mentoring traditional America provided. The good news is a trend is emerging to restore it.

My father ended up in a nursing home in our hometown of Portage, Wisconsin. He was in a wheelchair. I took time to attend chapel with him in the home, and after the service every person in the chapel walked over to shake his hand, greet him, and wish him well. After the chapel was empty, he looked at me and said, "Paul, isn't it great to be a family of honor." Yes, I saw in front of me the results of his and our mother's ethical, caring lives as members of the Portage community. Yes, dad, I want the honor too.

Dad's sister had stomach cancer, and she moved in to live with us. Her husband was dead; her only son, child had disowned her. One night, I woke up to voices downstairs. I sneaked down in my pajamas and stood aside in the dark. In the middle of the living room was my father on his knees. He was holding his sister, my aunt, on his lap while she was crying, "It's not fair. I'm to young to die. It's not fair." Yes, I "caught" a lesson from dad that night; if such a need ever arises again, I hope to live up to his example.

Again, voices in the middle of the night a couple of years later woke me. Once more, I was in my pajamas and standing in the dark downstairs while I watched my dad set another example for me. He was standing in the middle of the front door with the porch light on. He was saying, "No, she's not here. Go home now." In front of him was our big neighbor man who had been a floor security guard for Las Vegas casinos. He was no "piece of cake." Yet, my dad, a beautician, put himself between the "Mafioso" floor guard and his wife who was hiding in our basement. The neighbor man had just thrown his mother-in-law down a flight of stairs before trying to punch his wife, who was pregnant, in the face.

I wondered what was going to happen; suddenly, two police men emerged out of the dark to arrest the neighbor. I was relieved. Yet, I still admire the courage of my father to protect our pregnant neighbor friend at the risk of his own health – and maybe life. Yes, dad could comfort his dying sister; he also could ward off a drunken thug who sought to beat his pregnant wife. These are examples that set the standards for me to this day. They were "caught," not "taught." We can have both mercy and strength.

In mentoring, we can leverage such stories to ground us and mentoring partners in reality-based advice.

MENTORS: PRICELESS ADVISORS

PERSONAL APPLICATION: How does this case study remind you of mentoring events in your life? Please briefly cite five examples for possible discussion.

1.

2.

3.

4.

5.

CASE STUDY FIFTEEN: Irene Rux, Portage, Wisconsin

Like my father, my mother is an example of Aristotle's dictum about how our most important life's lessons are "caught" through, from the example of others, not taught through books of lectures. It is important to remember this as a guide to mentoring for both parties to the dialog. It can be powerful.

"I'm Wild Bill. I never worked and I never will." This was one of the favorite sayings of our neighbor boy, who was a year older than I am. Wild Bill, however, was retarded, or as we say today, had disabilities. As a result, his parents did their best to "hide" him so he would not distract or detract from the social status of his sister, Donna, who was four years older. If guests came to their home, they hid him upstairs or sent him to the movies. When it came time for him to go to school, Wild Bill went to St. John's Lutheran with me while his sister went to the public school. Since we lived nearby we got into the habit of walking to and from school together. This led to his becoming part of our family.

My mother replaced the love, care, and acceptance that he did not get from his own mother. In time, he became a regular at our house for breakfast and supper. My mother never once begrudged him or chided him for becoming one of us. He needed the love; she gladly gave it to him, an act of true mercy.

One day while he and I were playing together upstairs at our house, he stopped and looked at me. He had something to say. "God made me this way so you would appreciate what you have." I shall never forget this. There was more depth to Wild Bill than met the eye; my mother, a godly woman, saw it too.

When it came time for Confirmation in our Lutheran Church, Wild Bill was part of our group. He had done well with the basics of training in catechism and the Bible, even if the teachers simplified for him. Then, "hell broke loose." The pastor refused to confirm Wild Bill because he was retarded.

In turn, this ignited my mother, who immediately confronted the pastor over his refusal. She said, "Billy knows Jesus loves him; this is enough for him to be a full member of the church. In fact, if you refuse to confirm him, we will withdraw from the church and drop our membership."

This was powerful, for our family has always been devout Lutherans ever since immigrating from Germany. I even played the organ for services. The jolt from my mother go Wild Bill confirmed. I cannot think of a finer example of standing up for your faith, values, and disabled persons than this.

MENTORS: PRICELESS ADVISORS

My mother also practiced private charity. She identified poor families and found private ways to give them our surplus clothes as my brother, two sisters, and I grew out of them. I can still picture them coming to our house to try on the clothes. She even made special Christmas "packages" of clothing for the needy so they would have gifts to open on Christmas Eve. Mother set a powerful example for us.

Again, the power of example counts. We need to ask each other to share examples that have shaped our lives to gain better insight into each other, our strengths, and needs. Yes, leverage such examples to help to guide others to accept what they emotionally and intellectually know are right guides.

After his sister graduated from high school, the parents moved her and Wild Bill to Minneapolis/St. Paul All of them are deceased now; the example of how to and how not to treat each other remains for us.

PERSONAL APPLICATION: How does this case study remind you of mentoring events in your life? Please briefly cite five examples for possible discussion.

1.

2.

3.

4.

5.

CASE STUDY SIXTEEN: Christopher Holt, Toronto, Canada

Christopher is one of my two students whom I mentor for the University of Toronto. Christopher is pursuing his Ph.D., and Breanna Wu, the other student whom I mentor, is pursuing her M.S. Our formal format is to connect by phone or Skype for one hour monthly to mentor each other. Yes, mentoring is two-way exchange of information, support, and friendship. This differs from coaching and teaching which "top-down" approaches are in the final analysis. The letter below shows how mentoring differs.

May 11, 2018

TO: Christopher Holt

FROM: Dr. Paul Rux

RE: One-Hour Mentoring Session

Thank you, Christopher, for another excellent mentoring session. As you know, mentoring is two-way sharing. You share; I share. We both win! Thank you. We are acquiring a new, good, habit!

I am hopeful the University of Waterloo will hire you. You combine a unique blend of business achievement, academic excellence, and foresight. In addition, you know how to blend your "lessons

MENTORS: PRICELESS ADVISORS

learned" and insights from each of these fields to create exciting techniques to promote the good of others. Also, you have the energy to make an impact in and beyond Canada. It is exciting to know you!

I look forward to you email with the special websites for entrepreneurship. I also thank you for the update about major conferences yet this year in Chicago on entrepreneurship. They offer a good chance for us to visit in person, since I live three hours by car from downtown Chicago. Thanks for the offer!

As I shared, your campus-focused interest in entrepreneurship reminds me of my own work in this field back in 1990 in Westchester County, New York, where IBM has its international headquarters at Armonk. The difference is you have much more powerful experience, insight, and study to support you. In turn, your special blend of theory with practice will lead to stellar success! Please do what I missed.

Thank you also for your sharing how your daughter at Queen's University is reflecting on how to create "practical" applications for liberal arts, in her case, drama. As we discussed, the economy more and more will put pressure on persons who love liberal arts to find ways to earn livings with them. Again, you have foresight; you offer more than foresight. You also take practical steps because of foresight.

As we have done before, I am sharing a copy of this with Breanna Wu who is my other University of Toronto mentor. "Share the wealth." Thank you for sharing so much of yours with me today. Bravo!

I look forward to our next monthly mentoring session. If for some reason you need help from me in the interim, please feel free to ask for it. If I may need your help, I will also ask for it, too, as agreed.

Take care. I am proud to be your mentor and to have you as my mentor. Keep up your good work!

Dr. Paul Rux

608-471-2229 / paulrux@hotmail.com

PERSONAL APPLICATION: How does this case study remind you of mentoring events in your life? Please briefly cite five examples for possible discussion.

1.

2.

3.

4.

5.

CASE STUDY SEVENTEEN: Henry Menge, Montello, Wisconsin

Henry Menge was my mother's father. His values, courage, and skill helped to strongly shape the values of my mother directly and mine indirectly. Grandpa Menge had courage. He grew up on a farm, but he did not remain a farmer. Instead, he bought a chunk of farmland on the north shore of Lake Puckaway

MENTORS: PRICELESS ADVISORS

in Wisconsin. The Fox River, which connects the Wisconsin River with Lake Michigan runs through Lake Puckaway, and Grandpa Menge saw that the growing industrialization in Wisconsin as it entered the 1900's would result in metropolitan areas with persons who would pay good money for lakeside getaways to places like Puckaway. He really "hit the nail on the head" good and hard with his foresight.

Grandpa created Menge's Resort on the north shore of Lake Puckaway. It included a hotel, restaurant, tavern, cabins, hunting and fishing boat rentals. In addition, Grandpa Menge would mentor the city folks who wanted to fish and hunt but had no experience with it. In the process, he also taught my mother and her sister Arvilla how to run the business, which, in turn, prepared them for adult success.

Grandpa Menge also set a moral example for all of us. For instance, when he was building his resort, local Indians begged him not to dig in a certain area on his lakefront, for it contained an Indian burial ground. Grandpa agreed and left the graves untouched. He prevented violation of them "forever."

Grandpa Menge also purchased lakefront property on the Fox River which ran through Lake Puckaway. His lots sat on the river six miles outside Princeton, Wisconsin; Negroes from Milwaukee happened to be in the area on a visit and saw the for sale signs on the lots. They asked Grandpa to buy them. He agreed. Meanwhile, the white locals "raised hell" with him about letting black people move into the area. Grandpa stood his ground. He said, "Their money is as good as your money." This was a very powerful moral stand to take, and as with his Indian dealings, Grandpa always respected minorities.

Grandpa Menge also set another progressive example for his area. He bought a car so my mother could drive into Montello, Wisconsin to attend high school. She was the first girl to attend high school from the Puckaway area – ever – because of Grandpa's car for her; he also rented a room for her in Montello with family friends where she could overnight if bad weather made it dangerous to drive home in snow.

Grandpa's entrepreneurial spirit "rubbed off" on my mother; she attended beauty school in Milwaukee after graduating from high school. The result was her founding and operating three beauty shops all at once: Princeton, Montello, and Westfield. Her success convinced her boyfriend, who became her husband and my father, to attend beauty school also; she paid his way. Grandpa also bankrolled their first home.

The result was an income that put my mom and dad into a solid middle class lifestyle which opened the door to new opportunities for me and my siblings. Yes, the example, ethics, energy, entrepreneurship, and foresight of Grandpa Menge mentored us then, and it still does today. Like him, we still value equity and entrepreneurship. Thank you Grandpa Menge. We hope you are proud of us. Dr. Paul Rux

PERSONAL APPLICATION: How does this case study remind you of mentoring events in your life? Please briefly cite five examples for possible discussion.

1.

2.

3.

4.

5.

CASE STUDY EIGHTEEN: Dean Bowles, Ph.D., University of Wisconsin – Madison

Dean Bowles is on my list of exemplar mentors because he always wanted and listened to the "voice of the customer" in crafting services for others. I learned this through my first encounter with him as one of his Ph.D. students in research methods at Wisconsin-Madison.

To my delight, his course "boiled down" to an actual research project for the State of Wisconsin, which had launched a Wisconsin Scholars program to laud the state's top 100 high school graduates each year. The yearly winner received special award certificates, and then the program funded their four-year higher education costs after leaving high school.

However, to the surprise of the sponsoring bureaucrats in Madison, on average 50% of these Wisconsin Scholars chose to attend a college or university outside Wisconsin. How could this happen? They asked Bowles to use his research methods course to explore why 50% left Wisconsin after receiving one of the state's top scholarship awards? His course became a lab for applying research to the "real world."

Each course member got five Wisconsin Scholars from the recent spring award cycle to interview in person about how they made their choices for college and university education. It was classic market research. Listen to the "voice of the customer." The feedback from our field interviews, in turn, could help the Wisconsin Scholars program to help higher education recruit the 50% of the "best of the best" who left the state and rejected Wisconsin higher education each year.

Here are two examples of what I discovered during my field interviews. First, I went to Iowa to interview a young woman about her decision to leave Wisconsin. Her answer was, "As we walked through the dorms, I noticed empty liquor and beer bottles in many rooms. I did not want to try to study in the middle of a bunch of drunks." I agree. Iowa won; Wisconsin lost, rightly in this case.

Second, I interviewed a young man on leave from Colgate University in New York State. I asked him how Colgate became his choice, instead of some campus in Wisconsin. His answer was, "When students took me on tour of Wisconsin campuses most of them had no idea about the majors of their campuses. I did not want to be stuck in the middle of anti-intellectuals again. I got a belly full of that in high school."

Such feedback is priceless for admissions offices if they are interested in quality and not just quantity. Yes, listen to the "voice of the customer" if you want to serve them. The same logic applies to mentoring. As a mentor, we need to lisen to the "voices of the customers" whom we seek to serve if we want to connect with them and not have them reject us for somebody who respects their values.

Prof. Bowles taught me a memorable, priceless, hands-on lesson about communication, sales, mentoring, and healthy human relationships through his course. Given his mindset, I am not surprised he got elected to be Mayor of Monona, Wisconsin, the suburb of Madison, Wisconsin, where he lives, several times. This does not surprise me, for he hears the "voice of the voter" and responds to it.

MENTORS: PRICELESS ADVISORS

Prof. Bowles also has a gift for mentoring his students after they leave his classroom. For example, one of his students, Sondy Pope, is now my member of the Wisconsin State Assembly because of his mentoring. I also have been a member of the Madison West Rotary Club because of his mentoring. Madison West adjoins the University of Wisconsin campus and its membership draws heavily from the pool of professors there. Prof. Bowles felt my academic side needed nurturing. He got that right.

He and I share a passion for history, his B.A in history is from Yale, and mine is from Wisconsin-Madison. After Rotary meetings he and I would always linger to explore some aspect of history. In the process we would also find time for him to provide career mentoringas needed. He really knows how to mentor.

PERSONAL APPLICATION: How does this case study remind you of mentoring events in your life? Please briefly cite five examples for possible discussion.

1.

2.

3.

4.

5.

CASE STUDY NINETEEN: Donald J. McCarty, Ph.D., University of Wisconsin – Madison

Prof. McCarty was chair of my dissertation committee at Wisconsin – Madison. He held this position for the entire ten years it took for me to complete my Ph.D., which included a five-year leave of absence for me to recover my finances after my divorce. Prof. McCarty protected me during this process, which is a powerful example of his empathy as a mentor and courage to protect me from the system. During this long process we often had times when we were alone in his office; his sharing of insights was stellar.

For example, during one of our private office visits he looked at me across his desk and said, "Paul, you are different from the other students here. They want to be educators. You want to be a presidential advisor." Dr. McCarty taught politics of education, and he had managed political campaigns. He was not an amateur in politics; in fact, the Governor of Wisconsin, Tony Earl, was a surprise guest speaker for Dr. McCarty's politics course. Yes, McCarty could "read me" right. In fact, the president of a college in Kansas had offered me a job as his lobbyist in Washington, D.C. to "shake the money tree" for him. At the time, I could not take it; the skills and interest remained. McCarty could see and encouraged them.

Another "gem" of advice from him during one of our private meetings in his office was "Paul, in the end, it is always about budget." Again, he "hit the nail on the head" good and hard. He had been the Dean of the Wisconsin – Madison School of Education. **During World War II, he was a U.S. Army major who served on the staff of Supreme Allied Commander, later President, Dwight D. Eisenhower.**

MENTORS: PRICELESS ADVISORS

You do not fool persons with this kind of experience. It is priceless, and Dr. McCarty was willing to share it to help me to succeed as I moved into positions of power after my classroom theories were behind me. His mentoring was "short and sweet," but it summed up years of experience. I thank him for it.

PERSONAL APPLICATION: How does this case study remind you of mentoring events in your life? Please briefly cite five examples for possible discussion.

1.

2.

3.

4.

5.

CASE STUDY TWENTY: Breanna Wu, Toronto, Canada

Breanna Wu is one of my two grad students whom I mentor online, over the phone or Skype, for the University of Toronto. Breanna is age 32 and exploring the next steps in her career options. Below is our feedback to each other after our one-hour mentoring phone visit about her options . My summary of ourfirst mentoring visit about her options follows. After it comes her feedback to my feedback. This is a good example of personal mentoring between a "new" and an "old" practitioners in a career field.

March 13, 2018

"Breanna, here are my thoughts on your message below.

1. Yes, future focus counts. Wayne Gretzke said he was a great hockey player because he always focus on where the "puck is going" not where it is. This is an example of future focus. We do not want to "reinvent wheels" or play "catch up." At times we must. Ideally, we want to prepare ourselves to "skate to where the puck is going," so we become the "go-to experts" in demand. This puts us in demand, which, in turns, raises our value and what we can get paid.

2. As you know, in schools there are the classrooms and then there are the offices. Offices are the business centers for the school, which is a business, for it requires resources and hopefully gets results from cost-effective use of the resources. In the end, it all comes down to budget. ROI, return on investment, and at the top of all organizations to succeed must be ROI experts. I am not saying be an accountant. Rather, I am say, if you aspire to business make sure you focus on and document your capacity to generate ROI. Make sure, too, you write and speak about your ROI, which, in turn, positions you to transition to leading ROI in business. Whether we are in business or education, the challenge is to make the resources pay, produce outcomes of cost-effective values. This is especially true with private schools like UCC which cannot get tax welfare. If you want to position yourself for leadership in settings like UCC, they want ROI leaders.

MENTORS: PRICELESS ADVISORS

They also want leaders who know how to fund raise resources through gifts, grants, and know how to recruit and keep paying students. Yes, settings like UCC use business methods in order to survive and thrive. This is one reason such organizations appeal to you. Bravo!

Remember, also, public education also innovates with the creation of special schools, programs, resources, which requires a business person, not a bureaucrat who knows only how to play politics. Yes, we play politics in the private sector too, but to survive we must thrive, not play "games behind the curtain" in order to leverage tax funds, although we do some of this in the private sector. In short, as you compare education with business think budget, which means, ROI, return on investment. ROI applies in the final analysis to both business and education. In fact, you might pioneer a new approach to ROI approach to education as you specialty! I love this kind of blend of insights with foresight from different fields, disciplines, businesses. You could craft a career as a specialist in ROI as applied to education, which, in turn, bridges you into the business sector as well.

We also need to schedule a month, module two phone call yet this month. I am thinking some afternoon or evening during the last week of March would work best for me. Please share your thoughts. Also, make sure you send or resend the month two discussion foundation exercises before our phone sharing. Keep up your good work and enthusiasm! I love them! Dr. Rux"

Her reply follows below:

Breanna Wu <breanna.wu@mail.utoronto.ca>

Sun 3/11, 6:26 PM

"Thanks for your comments, Paul

For Educational Administration, could you please expand on that and how it links into business? My understanding of Educational Administration is educational leadership, so principals and superintendents would fall under that category - which are also two positions that would take years as a teacher to get into!

I'm going to brush up my CV and education (teaching) resume before reaching out to UCC! I'm thinking to include the two so they could learn a little about me as I'll reach out to ask about ways in which I could be involved. Now that I'm typing this out, it sounds kind of weird...

Thanks for connecting me to Dr. Sue Raftery! I'll reach out to her within the next few days!

Thank you for your feedback and thoughts! OD sounds a lot like a mix of things that I've explored a little in undergrad as well! I'll look into how that looks like in terms of jobs! Also thank you for your comment on my thoughtfulness about emergent trends, it's so rare nowadays to be... validated (for a lack of a better word in my brain right now) in such ways!

Breanna"

MENTORS: PRICELESS ADVISORS

PERSONAL APPLICATION: How does this case study remind you of mentoring events in your life? Please briefly cite five examples for possible discussion.

1.

2.

3.

4.

5.

CASE STUDY TWENTY-ONE: Tom McGonigle, Manhattan, New York City, New York

One of the key benefits of mentoring is the mutual sharing of information between persons. I am proud to say I have enjoyed such enriched mentoring since 1964 when I met my now lifelong friend and mentoring partner Thomas McGonigle. Tom war born and grew up on Long Island. As an adult he moved to live in the East Village on Manhattan Island in New York City, which he has remained still.

The core of our mentoring relationship is his sharing of insights from New York City where he lives with me, and my sharing of insights from the Midwest where I live. We have been doing this on a regular basis since 1964 when we met by surprise, in Dublin, Ireland, where both of us were university students for the 1964-1965 academic year.

The really funny twist to our meeting was both of us attended higher education in Wisconsin when we were not in Ireland. Tom was pursuing his B.A. at Beloit College there, and I was pursuing my B.A. at nearby University of Wisconsin – Madison. In Wisconsin we lived about forty miles apart; we did not meet until we went to Ireland! Some things are meant to be. Our mentoring friendship is one of them.

Tom was studying literature at the National University of Ireland, and I was studying history at the University of Dublin. I met Tom in the cafeteria at my university, for he would come there for better food and a larger mix of persons from different parts of the world who hung out in our cafeteria. In fact, later in our academic year, he and I received an invitation to appear on Irish National Television to discuss our impressions of Irish education. One of the first questions from the host was, "Tom, how did you get to meet Paul?" Tom answered, "In the cafeteria at his university." Both of us set aside the history of animosity between my campus, which was Protestant historically, and his campus, which was Catholic historically. It was great to brush aside years of hatred between campuses due to a cafeteria.

In fact, when I was flying home after my academic year in Ireland ended, the stewardess on our flight looked at me and said, "I saw you on TV, and I really had to laugh about how the campus cafeteria helped to heal years of historical religious strife at home in Ireland." Thank you for the kind comment.

MENTORS: PRICELESS ADVISORS

After returning to Wisconsin, Tom and I kept in touch. He would come to visit me in Madison; I would make trips to visit him in Beloit. However, Tom's roots were in New York City, and after he earned his B.A. from Beloit, he went home. Yet, we kept in touch; when I moved to New York City, 1998-2002, he and I reunited again. When we were unable to share thoughts with each other in person, we used the post office, telephone, and email. Tom shared the "Wall Street" New York perspective on events, and I shared how "red necks" in the Midwest interpreted events. Politics was a major focus of our sharing.

In 2008, I took my wife Jane for her first-ever visit to New York City. Of course, high on our "to-do" list on our trip was to meet with Tom and his wife, so the women could meet each other for the first time. They arranged a dinner for us at their fourth-floor, one-room, $3,000/month apartment on Third Street. They also invited their daughter and her finance. It was a big, new experience for Jane and me.

As usual, our conversation turned to how people in New York viewed events in comparison with how Midwesterners viewed them. In 2008, America was in the middle of a serve stock market crash, and since we were only three blocks from Wall Street for our get-together, it was only natural to share our perspectives on the financial crisis.

Tom asked his daughter and her fiancé to provide his perspective, since they both literally worked on Wall Street for powerful stock brokers. Their perspective, of course, was upbeat. The market crash was just a "bump in the road" and all would return to normal and go forward.

Then, he asked me what we in the Midwest thought about the Wall Street crash. I replied, "Yes, now we know there are really vampires on Wall Street." My answer resulted in a phone call from him the next morning about how my "vampires" answer really insulted his daughter and her fiancé, since they worked on Wall Street, literally. Wow, Tom provided honest feedback, and I offered honest apology.

I share this true Wall Street "vampire" event story as an example of how Tom and I have been honest with each other over the years in our exchange of insights, our mentoring of each other through New York City and Midwest "spins" on events. To his great credit, Tom was not going to let an oversight on my part derail our sharing, our mentoring of each other through sharing perspectives on persons and events. God bless Tom for the courage to heal this "vampire" comment and mentor me on why. I laud his polished politeness in how he brokered peace between me, his daughter and her finance. It is a stunning example of mentoring at its best, teaching others under stress in order to remove the stress.

Despite time, distance, and "vampires," Tom and I have maintained a loyal, caring mentoring friendship since 1964. I consider it to be one of the most rewarding achievements on my life path. Yes, from the start, we came from different backgrounds, but we have leveraged the differences to catalyze creative synergy to energize each other. When we are together, we are never bored. Our communications are never boring. From Tom, I have learned to take time, step back, listen to and consider another person's point of view. It is amazing how much we can learn this way. Thank you, Tom. Let's keep mentoring each other, amigo; again, thanks for your adroit defusing of the "vampire" dinner party incident.

MENTORS: PRICELESS ADVISORS

PERSONAL APPLICATION: How does this case study remind you of mentoring events in your life? Please briefly cite five examples for possible discussion.

1.

2.

3.

4.

5.

CASE STUDY TWENTY-TWO: Walter Froese, M.A., Barrie, Ontario, Canada

When I taught history and English at St. Andrew's College, Aurora, Ontario, Canada, and an elite prep boarding/day school for boys 1971-1972, I met Walter Froese, a new teacher also. He taught history, in which he had earned his M.A. from the University of Toronto, as had I. I was from Wisconsin, and he was from Manitoba. In effect, both of us were "outsiders" to Ontario and it was natural for us to find support from each other. This mutual support has continued after we left St. Andrew's in 1972 and continues to this day through emails and personal visits, in which we continue to mentor each other.

It is important to know that Walter immigrated with his mother to Manitoba from Germany after World War II after his father did not return from combat on the Russian front at the war's end. This gave Walter special, fresh, humane perspectives on events, and I still love his applying and sharing them.

Below, part A., is my reply on May 5, 2018, to the email from Walter, part B. In effect, we mentor each other as friends. It enriches our friendship and is an example of how mentoring can evolve over time.

  A. "Walter, you are a wonderful, gifted writer. Thank you for crafting and sharing this! It is very rich with insight. Look for ways to share your insight, wisdom with others. We need them badly. I hope you and yours are in good health. I just republished my UT thesis as a book on Amazon.com. I titled it: *Canadian Futurist: Thomas D'Arcy McGee*. It is now my second book on Amazon. *Hidden People* is first. I am working on my third now on mentoring, and I am halfway through it. We need to encourage each other to 'share the wealth' while we still have the ability to do it. Keep in touch. You are special. Paul"

  B. The following arrived from Walter by email on May 11, 2018. My response to him is A. above.

"Is it possible that Trump is what we needed at this stage in what we call western civilization?

I can't stomach the man but I also have serious reservations about the course the west has been following geopolitically and as a culture for decades now. Perhaps we need this iconoclast to shake things up in order for new things to take shape out of the apparent chaos. The danger does exist, as it did in the first part of the twentieth century, that we reap a whirlwind but perhaps we can do better this time.

MENTORS: PRICELESS ADVISORS

The two forces, entropy (chaos) and information (order) are always present. Briefly, this is the world 'order' in which I have been living:

* A small % of the world's population in the west representing roughly 20% of the world's population, consume 80% of the world's resources, based first on overt empire, and now through corporate power and global institutions.

* Within the 20%, the distribution of wealth has gradually centralized in less than 1% of the population.

* The digital revolution has outstripped our social institutions in adjusting to change so that everything from tax policy, employment, social discourse, crime, education appear chaotic. The old ways don't work in most jurisdictions.

* Our life expectancy has increased but much of that increase is prolonging death rather increasing quality of life.

* The nuclear family has exploded in the cult of the individual making individuals vulnerable when the social safety net fails. Symptoms include alienation, drug addiction, suicide and dystopic cult-like organizations.

* Consumer culture has enslaved large parts of the globe through cheap labour, imprisoned the consumer in instant gratification and polluted the planet to a point where even the fish can't breathe in our oceans.

* Humans are the dominant species in about 80% of the surface of our planet where we have displaced most vegetation with urban sprawl and with chemically induced monocultural agriculture and treats all non-human sentient beings as parts in an assembly plant.

* The imbalances humans have created in the ecosphere are only beginning to reveal consequences we can largely not control.

Facing the chaos approaching a century ago William Butler Yeats (1865-1939) wrote:

THE SECOND COMING

Turning and turning in the widening gyre

The falcon cannot hear the falconer;

Things fall apart; the centre cannot hold;

Mere anarchy is loosed upon the world,

The blood-dimmed tide is loosed, and everywhere

The ceremony of innocence is drowned;

The best lack all conviction, while the worst

MENTORS: PRICELESS ADVISORS

Are full of passionate intensity.

Surely some revelation is at hand;

Surely the Second Coming is at hand.

The Second Coming! Hardly are those words out

When a vast image out of Spiritus Mundi

Troubles my sight: a waste of desert sand;

A shape with lion body and the head of a man,

A gaze blank and pitiless as the sun,

Is moving its slow thighs, while all about it

Wind shadows of the indignant desert birds.

The darkness drops again but now I know

That twenty centuries of stony sleep

Were vexed to nightmare by a rocking cradle,

And what rough beast, its hour come round at last,

Slouches towards Bethlehem to be born?"

Perhaps the entropy induced by president Trump will inspire the 'best' to come forward and create a better "New Deal". There are some glimmerings that it may just happen.

For my granddaughters, I hope so"

Walter Froese

PERSONAL APPLICATION: How does this case study remind you of mentoring events in your life? Please briefly cite five examples for possible discussion.

1.

2.

3.

4.

5.

MENTORS: PRICELESS ADVISORS

CASE STUDY TWENTY-THREE: Sue Raftery, Ph.D., Norwalk, Ohio

I met Susan Raftery, Ph.D. (Ohio State University) in 2008 when she interviewed and hired me to become part of the new online DBA (Doctor of Business Administration) program for the new online university, Jones International University, which opened in 1999. In less than ten years, its appeal to online students enabled it to launch an online DBA program, and in 2008, I interviewed with Dean Susan Raftery for a teaching job in the new DBA program. Raftery had set up the program for Jones, and she knew exactly what kind of teachers they needed to jumpstart the program and make it a success.

She liked my online background, which began in 1998 on a non-stop basis. I offered 10 years of B.A. and M.B.A. teaching and course design experience and was ready for the next logical professional career step, teaching DBA students and designing courses for them. Raftery hired me, and I grew personally and professionally with Raftery's upbeat mentoring of me with Jones from 2008-2015.

Sadly enrollment fell; Jones closed in 2015. Nonetheless, my seven years with Jones enabled me to take my next teaching career step, the teaching of doctoral students and the design of courses and programs for them. I now apply the "lessons learned" to other online teaching opportunities with confidence.

Jones also enabled me to benefit from the mentoring of Dr. Susan Raftery, which has led to a professional and personal friendship beyond the close of Jones in 2015. Yes, I gained great value from my time at and work for Jones. I also, more importantly, during the process gained a stellar lifetime mentor and friend who still provides grounded professional, personal support for me as I ask her for it.

At heart, Raftery is an impressive entrepreneur. As Jones closed, she launched a project to create greenhouses with training centers on how to use them across the U.S. She mentored me on how she had to lobby various levels of government and to market her concept at state, national, and even international trade shows. Funding for greenhouses, of course, was a major challenge, and it in time caused her to change career direction, start and operate an online jounal on agricultural technological innovation. The cost of a website is much, much less than a greenhouse with a training center.

Sue is creative, but she also is pragmatic and respects limits to time, health, energy, and opportunities. She knows when to quit; she also knows when to start. I thank her for discussing such decisions with me. It is a first-class form of mentoring.

My wife and I, moreover, thank her for invitations for us to come to Ohio to visit Amish country in Northeastern Ohio, which is on her doorstep. This gives us time to get to know each other as persons, not just professionals, a perfect mixture for mentoring.

Sue Raftery has mentored me about formal academics, entrepreneurship, and how to stay healthy doing them. She shares precious "lessons learned" to help me "stay afloat." Whenever I can, I share "lessons learned" from my life path to encourage and enable her to continue to sculpt the future.

Yes, learning from each other is at the heart of mentoring; encouraging each others is also at its heart too. Sue Raftery and I have been able to craft a friendship in which such mentoring is now ongoing.

MENTORS: PRICELESS ADVISORS

PERSONAL APPLICATION: How does this case study remind you of mentoring events in your life? Please briefly cite five examples for possible discussion.

1.

2.

3.

4.

5.

CASE STUDY TWENTY-FOUR: Louis Menge, Montello, Wisconsin, World War I "Doughboy"

On the wall in my study hangs a picture frame with a glass covering. Behind the glass are military patches from World War I which my grandpa Henry Menge's brother Louis Menge wore on duty. I am honored to be the guardian of his shoulder patches, for they continue to mentor me about what is of value for him and me. His story about his combat experience in the "Great War" has shaped my values.

Uncle Louis was a mechanic in rural Wisconsin when President Woodrow Wilson drafted him and sent him to war in France. Because of his mechanical skills, Uncle Louis ended up in providing trucks to haul supplies to the frontline combat forces and to haul wounded American soldiers back from the fighting to aid stations. One day in France, a fierce frontline battle erupted and Uncle Louis and his comrades loaded their trucks with ammunition and haulted it to help our frontline fighting forces to survive.

After unloading the ammunition, they would return to refill their trucks with more of it. On the drive back they would encounter our wounded soldiers making their ways, as best they could, back from the battle front to medical aid stations behind the lines. Uncle Louis and his comrades would stop to load their trucks with these wounded American soldiers, many of whom could not walk any longer, and haul them back for medical help.

During this battle, an officer -- with a drawn pistol -- came up to Uncle Louis and his fellow drivers who were loading our wounded and said, "The ammunition is more important. Do not stop to pick up the wounded, or risk the consequences."

Uncle Louis and his comrades, as a result, ended up driving over their own wounded who would beg them not to kill them. At day's end, Uncle Louis and his comrades had to clean the body parts and blood of our own soldiers off their trucks.

As a result, Uncle Louis resolved to never let anybody ever again draft him into a war. The forced murder of his own soldiers haunted him for the rest of his life. His story also has mentored me about war and has been a key reason why I am a conscientious objector.

Out of respect for Uncle Louis, when I was in Washington, D.C., I went to the National Cathederal, where President Woodrow Wilson is buried.

MENTORS: PRICELESS ADVISORS

I walked over to his grave and said, "Louis Menge sends his regards and his anger that you caused America to enter a needless war -- and forced him to kill our own people by drafting him into it.

We're still here you 'S.O.B.'" I share the values of Uncle Louis. Thank you Uncle Louis for your courage to tell us what happened to you in World War I. It has guided me well.

PERSONAL APPLICATION: How does this case study remind you of mentoring events in your life? Please briefly cite five examples for possible discussion.

1.

2.

3.

4.

5.

<u>**CASE STUDY TWENTY-FIVE**</u>: **Paul Rux, Ph.D., 405 Lake St., Mt. Horeb, WI 53572 (paulrux@hotmail.com) Phone: 608-471-2229.**

"Lessons Learned" from My First Mentoring Job

My first experience with working as a formal mentor took place during my high school teaching career. I was on the faculty of an upscale coed boarding junior/senior high school in the Midwest, which sought to enroll 300 students each year to make ends meet.

However, for myriad reasons, by the end of the first semester, which ended with Christmas vacation, the school lost on average half of the 300 students who had enrolled at the start of the school year for re-enrollment in its second semester at the start of the New Year.

In short, the school faced collapse if it did not reverse this dropout rate; one way it chose to do this was to apply mentoring. Each teacher became a mentor to five students at the start of the school year and performed this function through the school year. This was in addition to high teaching expectations.

This is how it worked. Each teacher became mentor to five students from his or her teaching grade level. This was in addition to our full-time classroom teaching load. Here are our mentoring duties:

1. We had to meet privately with each of the five students in our mentor group each week to ascertain how they were or were not progressing, why, and what to do about it.

2. Our duties as mentors included serving as a student advocate during any disciplinary actions. In short, we became "trial defense attorneys" for the five students in our mentor group. The "trials" were last-minute efforts to retain students and avoid malpractice lawsuits against the school for collection tuition for the school year while expelling a student during the school year without any financial reimbursement.

MENTORS: PRICELESS ADVISORS

The stress of this mentoring in a setting where half of the students quit or got kicked out by mid-year was too great on me. After three years, I left to take a job as a public school library director. From there, I got my doctorate and went into higher education, lobbying, and business.

Now, as a specialist in management, I realize my first mentoring experience at the boarding school taught some valuable insights into mentoring as I reflect on them as follows:

1. Yes, it pays to work with persons on a one-to-one basis. However, if we observe a toxic misfit between the people whom we are mentoring with the organization, we need to have the ethical courage to say so and explore exit remedies, which includes constructive excites and alternatives. In my example of the boarding school, it was keep the student tuition at all costs, regardless of the damage to the student and organization. This is not ethical mentoring. Say yes or no.

2. Mentoring is not a "magic bullet" to make everybody fit into every situation. Ethical mentoring knows how to "say no" to situations for our clients and suggest constructive exits and options. for such toxic mismatches. I believe such advice is ethical mentoring at its very best always.

For the record, the last information about this school to come my way said it now has students from thirty-three different countries! It is prospering. By restoring its legacy of learning excellence, academic and social, it is surviving the collapse of the American middle class from which it once only got students.

Someday, I would like to revisit the school to review how it does or does not apply mentoring. I hope it does, for if it helps students to learn, mature, and self-actualize it is a great asset. If it is only a "bag of tricks" to get tuition at any costs, it is toxic. I suspect the success of the school now with enrollment means its mentoring is about students, not money. It is great to get news like this. We need more of it! share this case study as a reminder of how ethical mentoring ought to work. Nothing beats experience.

PERSONAL APPLICATION: How does this case study remind you of mentoring events in your life? Please briefly cite five examples for possible discussion.

1.

2.

3.

4.

5.